Surviving the

MARATHON DES SABLES

AN INTERACTIVE EXTREME SPORTS ADVENTURE

Matt Doeden

raintree

a Capstone company — publishers for children

Raintree is an imprint of Capstone Global Library Limited, a company incorporated in
England and Wales having its registered office at 264 Banbury Road, Oxford, OX2 7DY –
Registered company number: 6695582

www.raintree.co.uk
myorders@raintree.co.uk

Edited by Nate LeBoutillier
Designed by Bobbie Nuytten
Picture research by Eric Gohl
Production by Katy LaVigne
Originated by Capstone Global Library Limited
Printed and bound in China

ISBN 978 1 47474 367 9
21 20 19 18 17
10 9 8 7 6 5 4 3 2 1

British Library Cataloguing in Publication Data
A full catalogue record for this book is available from the British Library.

Acknowledgements
We would like to thank the following for permission to reproduce photographs: Getty Images:
Jean-Philippe Ksiazek, 18, 33, 49, 54, Pierre Verdy, 4, 93, 98, 103, Stringer/AFP, 12, 100;
iStockphoto: GavinD, 72, Pavliha, 21, 106 (bottom); Newscom: Icon SMI/Christophe Dupont
Elise, 10, 27, 38, 44, 46, 74, 84, 91, 96; Shutterstock: acceptphoto, 59, Christoph Lischetzki,
68, Dudarev Mikhail, cover, Galyna Andrushko, 41, Greta Gabaglio, 77, GulOnder, 1,
HandmadePictures, 15, James Carnegie, 81, M.Khebra, 62, 107 (top), Marques, 6, 106 (top),
Protasov AN, 107 (bottom)

CONTENTS

ABOUT YOUR ADVENTURE

YOU are about to take part in one of the most difficult, physically demanding races in the world.

The Marathon des Sables is an endurance challenge that spans 251 kilometres (156 miles) through the heart of one of the world's most inhospitable climates, the Sahara Desert. The choices that you make will guide the story and determine your fate. How will you run the race? Will you make your way with caution in mind or charge ahead for glory? Can you manage your resources and health well enough to actually cross the finish line?

Turn the page to begin your adventure.

CHAPTER 1

WELCOME TO MOROCCO

The Moroccan sun beats down on the sand. You wipe a trail of sweat from your brow as you pull on your running shoes. After three days of travel, more airport food than you ever want to eat again and a bus ride over rough desert roads, you feel hot and exhausted already ... and the race hasn't even begun. But you're here at the Marathon des Sables, "the marathon of the sands".

You glance around at the hundreds of runners preparing for the first leg of the six-day, 251-kilometre race. Old and young. Men and women. People from many different nations. You've spent most of your time since arriving in Morocco just meeting people and making friends.

Turn the page.

When you found out that your older twin siblings, Mona and RJ, had decided to travel to the Sahara Desert to run the Marathon des Sables, you begged them to let you come. After all, you already know you can beat either of them in any footrace. Weeks of prodding, hinting and working over your parents finally paid off.

Mona grins at you as she checks her rucksack. "At least it's a dry heat, eh?" she says.

You can't help but chuckle.

"You ready, kid?" It's Andrew. You sat by him on the bus ride out here. He's old enough to be your dad, but here in the middle of the desert, it doesn't seem to matter as much. He just feels like a friend. His daughter, Haley, is by his side.

"Can anyone ever be ready for this?" you reply. "How are you, Haley?"

"Nervous?" she says. "Excited? Terrified? Not sure which. Maybe all."

You can't help but admire her. Haley, who's just a few years older than you, is blind. As hard as this race is for someone who can see, you can't imagine what it will be like for her.

Over Haley's shoulder you spot Gunther and Zelig stretching. They're German runners and serious competitors. Most of the people here just want to finish the race. Gunther and Zelig are among the few here that will try to win it.

Gunther gives you a wave. "The offer is still open,' he calls out in his German accent. Gunther and Zelig had said that you were welcome to run with them if you think you can keep up. You're not sure if they really want you along, but you can't help but feel proud that they even asked.

Turn the page.

Runners check in with administrators before racing and must carry their own food, sleeping gear and other materials.

Mona gives you a stern look. "Don't even think about it," she warns. "You're not ready for that." She's probably right. And she means well. But just the fact that she says it sort of makes you want to try anyway.

As the start of the race draws near, all of the runners make their final preparations. Their supplies are packed. Their bags are strapped to their backs. And the carefree attitude of the place takes on a more serious tone.

"What do you say, kid?" Zelig asks. You look from him to your siblings to Andrew and Haley. Who you run with may be the single most important decision of the entire race. The choices cycle through your mind. What is it you hope to get out of the Marathon des Sables? Is it a shot to compete at the highest level? An opportunity to spend the race with someone overcoming tremendous odds? Or a rare chance to spend some quality time with Mona and RJ?

"I'm coming," you call out, jogging over to the group you'll spend the race with.

To run with Gunther and Zelig, turn to page 13.

To stay with Mona and RJ, turn to page 47.

To choose Andrew and Haley, turn to page 75.

CHAPTER 2

BLAZING A TRAIL

Gunther gives you a broad smile and an encouraging slap on the back as you join their group. "Glad to have you," he says. "I just hope you're ready. We set a steady pace, and we don't slow down."

You strap on your rucksack. It contains all of your food and your first ration of water. And with that, the race begins. As competitive racers, Gunther and Zelig take off from near the front of the pack. Other groups stream out behind. In the early parts of the race, this must look like some great animal migration, with runners following in a densely populated line through the desert.

Turn the page.

At first, their pace doesn't seem all that fast to you. You don't have any trouble keeping up. But as you approach the first of a series of tall sand dunes, you start to realise that this isn't just any marathon. You haven't even gone one kilometre yet, but the sand is everywhere. It's in your shoes, in your hair and in your eyes. As Gunther and Zelig charge up a dune, you have to reach deep down inside yourself just to keep up.

And so it goes for about 12 kilometres. Up and down the dunes. The pack of racers spreads out. Your group is near the front. As the sun rises higher and higher in the sky, sweat pours down your face. You reach again and again for the water that your body craves.

"Slow down on the water," Gunther warns, the first words any of you have spoken since the first stage began. "You don't want to run out."

To your dismay, he doesn't even sound out of breath. Your own lungs scream for more oxygen.

At first, you try to follow his advice. But in no time, you're guzzling your water again. You swallow the last drop a little more than halfway through the stage. Luckily, one of the race's many checkpoints stands not too far up ahead along the path.

In the Sahara Desert, water is the most precious of commodities.

Turn the page.

The checkpoints, set every 10 kilometres, always offer the chance for medical assistance, as well as for water.

"I need more water," you huff to one of the workers at the station. It's a middle-aged woman who appears to be native to Morocco. She replies in perfect English. "You can have more water, of course. But taking more than your daily ration will result in a time penalty."

Your heart sinks. Not even one day in and you'd already be taking a penalty, hurting your hopes of posting a winning time with your new friends.

To take the water and the penalty, turn to page 17.
To keep going without additional water, turn to page 32.

The desert sun is brutally hot, and it's only getting hotter. "Okay," you sigh. "I don't have much choice."

As you sip on your new stash of warm water, you know that you made the right decision.

"Good luck the rest of the way," says the worker, giving you a smile. "I hope you make it!"

You mutter a thank you and resume your pace. Gunther and Zelig are distant dots on the horizon now, their figures hazy through the waves of hot air. Soon, they climb over a dune and you lose sight of them on the other side. You don't see them again for several hours, at the end of the stage. By the time you hobble across the finish line, they've already changed clothes, eaten some food and settled into one of the race's many burlap tents.

Turn the page.

Zelig spots you and shouts out your name. "You made it! Well done, my young friend. How do you feel?"

"Great," you lie. In truth, you're exhausted. You feel light-headed, and your feet ache. Pulling off your shoes and socks reveals several large blisters. You're so tired the pain hardly registers.

Competitors may receive treatment for their feet at different stages of the race.

As more and more runners finish the stage, the small community of tents grows. Soon, it is buzzing with excitement. Runners eat, drink and laugh together. You cheer on Mona and RJ as they finish the first stage, greeting each with a hug.

In time, you collapse in your tent. You sleep hard. When you wake up, you're stiff and sore but ready to go. Gunther and Zelig are already lacing their shoes and strapping their packs. By the time the second stage starts, the aches and pains are long forgotten.

You keep up for a few kilometres before drifting back again. This time, it doesn't bother you. Keeping pace with world-class athletes is a lofty goal. Just staying close is victory enough. You find yourself staring off onto the horizon as you fall into a rhythm. A line of footprints in the sand marks a clear path to the next checkpoint.

Turn the page.

You squint as a strange, dark mass seems to rise up over the desert.

"What is that?" you mutter to yourself.

The darkness grows and grows. The wind begins to howl. And before you realise what's happening, a raging sandstorm eclipses the sky. In an instant, you are thrown into a whirling, swirling darkness. Sand stings your face. The wind pushes against your body. Panic sets in.

To get down and cover yourself, turn to page 21.
To push on through the sandstorm, turn to page 24.

Blowing and swirling sand fills the air. These storms are common in the Sahara, and you know from research that they generally don't last long. The best thing you can do is to protect yourself. You pull your shirt up over your face and huddle on the ground.

Sandstorms in the Sahara can be massive and can totally rearrange the landscape.

Turn the page.

The wind blows on and on.

Minutes creep by, but in time the sandstorm weakens. Then, as quickly as it came, it's gone. You stand up and look around. The landscape has been reshaped. The trail of footprints in the sand has been wiped away. Thankfully, you have your compass, which you use to get back on track. Soon, you come over a rise to see the next checkpoint in the distance.

"Are you okay?" one of the race workers shouts out as you approach.

You nod. "Crazy out there," you add.

To your surprise, Gunther and Zelig are still at the checkpoint. One of Zelig's feet is bare. He's picking at a particularly nasty blister. It's oozing blood and pus. The sight of it makes your stomach lurch. You quickly look away.

"He's not going to be able to keep going," Gunther says with a sigh. "At least not at the kind of pace I'll need to compete."

"What are you going to do?" you ask.

Gunther shrugs. "I'll press on. I can run alongside some of the other competitive racers, I suppose."

"You should run with him," Zelig offers. "Go in my place."

Gunther gives a thin smile. "I think our young friend would be better served sticking with you, Zelig. You'll be running a slower pace with that foot."

Both men look at you.

To run the rest of the way with Gunther, turn to page 30.
To stick with Zelig, turn to page 36.

You came out here to take on the elements. Well, this is your chance. You pull your shirt up over your mouth and nose to use as a breathing filter and then press on. The wind whips you, and the sand blasts you. But you keep putting one foot in front of the other.

The minutes tick by agonizingly. Your eyes are dry and itchy. Your back is sore from bracing against the wind. Yet as you continue forward, almost blindly, the storm begins to weaken. And then, just like that, the sandstorm is over.

You stand, hands on hips, taking deep, clean breaths of hot, dry desert air. You scan the horizon. Nothing looks familiar. You've strayed off the main course. Which way is the next checkpoint? You think back to your training. Mona always said that if you get separated from the pack, just shout at the top of your voice.

Sound carries well across the barren desert and someone is bound to hear you. But the thought of standing here crying for help just seems so embarrassing. Ahead stands a rocky rise. That might be right. If you can get to higher ground, maybe you'll be able to see something. But it's a long way up there. If it's the wrong way, you'll lose a lot of time.

To shout out for help, turn to page 26.
To head for the higher ground, turn to page 38.

No good can come of striking out into the desert blind. You know that you can't have wandered far off course. Other runners must be near, even if you can't see them.

"Help!" you shout. "Anyone, help!"

It doesn't take long before you hear a woman's voice call back. "Hello? Where are you?"

You call back and forth for several minutes, following along a low, rocky ridge towards the sound of the voice. Finally, beyond the ridge, you spot a group waving. You breathe a huge sigh of relief as you greet them with warm handshakes. It's a Brazilian group that has been sticking near the middle of the pack.

"I'm Ana Luiza," says a woman who appears to be in her thirties. She's the only one in the group who speaks your language.

In any language, these are your kind of folks. They laugh and joke throughout the rest of the stage, occasionally breaking out into song in their language. One of them, Paulo, runs the leg with a pair of underpants on his head. You even pick up a few new words along the way, joining in on the songs and singing all the lyrics in a way that makes everyone laugh.

Turn the page.

Most Marathon des Sables competitors run in groups.

Ana Luiza sets a comfortable pace. It's nice not having to push yourself so hard. By the time you reach the stage's finish line, you have a whole new group of friends, even if you can't speak directly to most of them.

You meet up with Gunther at the tent. Zelig is at the medical tent getting attention for a terrible blister. Gunther is afraid that his friend might not be able to continue. As the two of you discuss the situation, Mona and RJ spot you and rush over to check on you. Gunther goes to get an update on Zelig while you tell them about your adventure with the sandstorm.

"Maybe it's time to hang back and run with us," Mona suggests, looking concerned. "It doesn't seem like you're quite ready to run with the German fellows."

You hate to bail on your friends, but Mona has a point. You have to admit that.

You got lucky – today could have been much worse. But you're not sure you can resist the chance to run with a competitive racer.

To continue with Gunther, turn to page 30.
To finish the race with Mona and RJ, turn to page 50.

The next day, you and Gunther stand at the starting line, ready to run. Zelig, hobbling on his blistered foot, wishes you luck.

"It's just you and me, kid," Gunther says as the stage begins. The two of you set out at a brisk pace. Guther is relentless. Every time you think he might tire, he pushes forward. He's a marvel to watch. Every step is filled with purpose, and he never allows himself to slow down. There's no doubt he's hurting almost as much as you are, but you'd never know it from his effortless stride. It's an inspiration, driving you to do the same.

It's the hottest day yet. You're desperate for water, but you manage your ration carefully. Step by step, you cross the desert sands and salt flats. You lose track of the time. You barely even notice the other runners around you. All that matters is the next step.

"Keep it up," Gunther says, pointing ahead. "Just a few more kilometres to go. Let's push to the finish!"

With that, Gunther picks up the pace. You try to match it, but your calves feel like they're about to explode. Your lungs burn. Gunther outpaces you by ten steps … twenty steps. Your heart feels like it's about to beat out of your chest. You want to keep up the pace and push yourself to the limit, but you're not sure you could even muster the breath to call out and ask him to slow down.

To conserve your energy and fall back, turn to page 41.
To push harder and try to keep up, turn to page 43.

There's no way you're taking a time penalty this early in the race. You ran with this group because you wanted to see what it would take to compete at the highest level.

Going over your water ration on the very first stage and having to pay for it with a penalty isn't exactly the way to do that.

"No, I'm okay," you tell the woman. "Thanks, anyway."

She raises an eyebrow. "Are you sure? It's only getting hotter out here."

Not long after you blow through the checkpoint, you realise that the woman was right. The sun continues to rise in the sky. The heat rises off the desert sands, distorting the light and making you feel dizzy. But you've made your decision and try to stay strong.

Village children occasionally greet
competitors in the Marathon des Sables.

The stage takes you over stony ground, past a
small Moroccan village. Gunther and Zelig keep
up their pace, but you slowly drift back half a
kilometre or more.

Some of the village children cheer you on
as you pass by. Their support gives you a boost,
and once again you pick up your pace. The gap
between you and your new friends closes.

Turn the page.

Without thinking, you reach for your water bottle. Of course, it's empty. You shake it to rattle out a few final drops. But it's not nearly enough. You stop for a moment, putting your hands on your knees, trying to catch your breath.

When you stand upright again, the world begins to spin. Darkness creeps around the edges of your vision, and your knees go weak. You collapse onto the stony ground, knocking your head on a sharp rock.

"Medic!" someone shouts.

Your world goes dark . . .

You wake up in a medical tent with an IV in your arm. A young man looks down at you, taking your blood pressure.

"You pushed yourself too hard and passed out after hitting your head," he explains. "Dehydration and heat stroke are huge dangers out here, and you're suffering from both. Next time, take it slower."

"Next time?" you mumble, trying to stand. "What do you mean next time?"

The young man puts a hand on your shoulder. "Sorry, kid," he says. "Your race is over. Maybe next time you'll be more careful out there."

THE END

To follow another path, turn to page 11.
To learn more about the Marathon des Sables, turn to page 101.

Gunther is right. You should stick with Zelig. The two of you wave at your friend as he takes off. You wait with Zelig as he gets medical attention for his blister. Within an hour, the two of you are back on the course, navigating a rough, rocky climb. The slower pace you're at because of Zelig's blister drops you back with many of the less experienced racers. You even get the chance to run with your brother and sister for a few kilometres.

Over the next five days, you and Zelig stick it out. He's in a lot of pain. But so is almost everyone in this wild race.

You don't see much of Gunther the rest of the way, except on the race's lone day of rest. He stays near the front. Meanwhile, it takes you and Zelig from sunrise to past sunset just to complete several of the stages.

But for all the aches and pains, you wouldn't change a thing. As you and Zelig limp across the finish line together – many hours behind the winners, but far ahead of both of your siblings – you feel an intense wave of pride.

"Congratulations," calls Gunther, who is there to cheer you both on. The three of you hug, and you know you've found friends for life.

"What do you say?" Zelig says. "Should we try it again next year?"

You can't wipe the smile off your face.

THE END

To follow another path, turn to page 11.
To learn more about the Marathon des Sables, turn to page 101.

There's no time to waste. You adjust your pack and head for high ground. The rocky ground is covered in sand. The footing is bad, and several times you nearly slip and fall. But you're careful and determined. You finally reach the high point of the rise and scan your surroundings.

Some of the most daunting slopes are outfitted with guide cords for runners' safety.

All you see is desert. No checkpoints, no route markers. No other runners. You're out here all alone, and you've clearly gone in the wrong direction.

You shout for help, but no one can hear you. So you do the only thing you can do. You pick a direction and start walking. For the entire afternoon, you trudge over the desert sands, unsure if you're even heading the right way. The sun is dipping low in the sky when you finally spot something in the distance – a thin trail of footprints in the sand.

You let out a whoop of joy and sprint to the tracks. From there, you easily navigate your way towards the stage's finish line.

The sky has gone completely dark when you finally check in.

Turn the page.

"I'm sorry," says a young man who welcomes you. "You didn't make it before the cut-off time. I'm afraid your race is over."

You drop to a knee as though kicked in the stomach. The words keep going through your head. *Your race is over . . .*

Your goal was simple – to finish. And, you didn't even manage to get through one stage.

THE END

To follow another path, turn to page 11.
To learn more about the Marathon des Sables, turn to page 101.

You just can't do it. You don't want to push your body any further. You stop, bent over at the waist, and watch as Gunther disappears off into the distance. Several other runners pass you by as you stand there.

Turn the page.

The Sahara provides a beautiful – and desolate – landscape.

"Hey, don't give up now," says one young man. "Come on, run with us!"

You try. But after less than a kilometre, you feel like they're going too fast for you too. You settle into a slow walk instead. With every step, you notice the pain in your feet and legs more and more. Your calves start cramping. Feeling completely spent, you slump down in the desert sand, sobbing.

Somehow you manage to make your way to the next checkpoint. But that's it for you. The Marathon des Sables has broken you. It's time to go home.

THE END

To follow another path, turn to page 11.
To learn more about the Marathon des Sables, turn to page 101.

You've come this far. You can't bear the thought of falling back now. So you dig deep. You tap into reserves of energy and willpower that you didn't even know that you had.

As you bound forwards, the gap between Gunther and you shrinks … and shrinks … and shrinks. With a surge, you speed ahead of him.

"Try to keep up," you huff over your shoulder.

The two of you finish the stage side by side with one of the best times in the entire race. "I didn't know I had it in me," you say in disbelief.

Gunther smiles. "I knew," he whispers.

And so you continue the race. Now that you know what you're capable of, you don't let anything stand in your way. After the sixth gruelling leg, you cross the finish line.

Turn the page.

The sight of the end of a stage at the Marathon des Sables is a thing of beauty – and relief.

Even with the water penalty you took, you have the best time of any racer under the age of 20. The celebration is on. Your friends shower you with congratulations. You get hugs from Ana Luiza, Haley and both of your siblings. Complete strangers shake your hand and offer you smiles and hugs.

It's one of the greatest feelings of your life. You came to the Sahara, and you conquered the gruelling Marathon des Sables.

THE END

To follow another path, turn to page 11.
To learn more about the Marathon des Sables, turn to page 101.

CHAPTER 3

FAMILY FIRST

You came half way around the world to do this with your brother and sister. And while making new friends is great, you want to spend your time with your family.

The three of you start the race together, keeping a slow but steady pace. You don't have any delusions about winning. Your goal is simple – to finish the race. To do that, all you have to do is finish each stage before the cut-off time. With a steady pace, you know that won't be a problem.

The first two days take you through the heart of the desert. You run over huge, rolling sand dunes and rocky terrain. The heat is intense.

Turn the page.

You're careful about rationing your supplies.

"Makes me think of when you were little," Mona remembers, watching you take tiny sips. "Mum and Dad wouldn't let you drink more than a couple of sips of water before bed. Once I gave you a whole glass, and you wet your bed that night. They made me clean it up!"

RJ bursts out laughing. Soon, they're both chuckling away, and your face is red with embarrassment. But that doesn't last long. Soon, you're laughing right along with them. And you're glad you decided to stick with them.

During the evenings, you enjoy the company of the other runners. Everyone sleeps in open burlap tents. They form a small city of runners every night. Despite the aches, pains and general exhaustion, you're enjoying the race.

Tents between stages of the Marathon des Sables provide runners much-needed climate protection and rest.

You spot Gunther that night. He and Zelig are keeping pace with the leaders.

"You should have run with us, kid," he says with a smile. "It's not too late!"

Turn the page.

You give Gunther a grin. "I think running with Mona and RJ is the right choice for me," you explain.

Gunther winks at you and heads off to find Zelig. "I will see you at the finish line, my friend," he calls back.

The third stage will be the longest yet. You're at the starting line at the break of dawn. The desert air is cool at present, but you're well aware that it won't stay that way for long. It's going to be the hottest day yet.

The stage starts out flat, but you're soon facing a series of rocky jebels. These small mountains rise above the desert sands. As you begin to climb the first of them, your calves begin to strain.

"Hey, I think you have a new friend there," RJ calls out.

"What?" you answer.

You glance back over your shoulder. A small, scrawny dog is bounding along at your heels. You pull up and extend a hand for the little terrier to sniff. He licks you and pushes his head into your palm.

"He wants you to pet him," Mona says. All three of you stop, gathering around the friendly little dog. A few other runners from another group stand and watch as well.

"Where do you belong, little fella?" you ask.

The dog just pants. As it breathes, you can see the shape of its ribs through its matted fur.

Turn the page.

"You're so skinny," you say.

The dog turns its eyes to you and licks its lips.

You've got a bit of beef jerky in your pack. You're tempted to give some to the dog. However, you've carefully counted out every calorie you need, so anything you give him is energy you won't have for yourself.

To feed the dog, turn to page 53.
To conserve your supplies for yourself, turn to page 56.

You can't resist sharing a bit of your food with the dog. "Here you go, little fella," you say, snapping a stick of beef jerky in half and letting him take it from your hand. The dog sniffs at it and then eagerly gobbles it up.

"What is it with you and animals?" RJ asks. "Remember that summer when we had like four stray cats living on our doorstep?"

It's true. You've always loved animals. It seems like this little dog must have sensed that somehow. You pet the dog one last time. "Okay, go home!" you command. But the dog doesn't do that. Instead, it follows you. As you wind through the desert and over a series of tough climbs, the dog is your constant shadow.

"That's exactly what you should call him," Mona jokes. "Shadow."

Turn the page.

It's a difficult day. All three of you are suffering from blisters on your feet. You barely make it across the finish line before the cut-off time. At camp, you and Shadow quickly become celebrities. Everyone adores the little pup and offers him bits of food. Shadow never lets you out of his sight. He even sleeps at your feet.

The time between stages provides competitors with a chance to socialize and recover.

Stage four begins early. Your group of three –
now four – strikes out as the sun hangs low over the
Sahara's eastern horizon. The jebels slowly give way
to more rolling sand dunes.

About halfway through the leg, Mona asks for a
break. "Let's just sit a few minutes," she says.

A group of rocks just off the course offer a place
to sit. You make your way towards the rocks, but
before you can sit, Shadow starts to growl.

"Settle down, boy," you say. "We're just taking
a rest."

Shadow lets out a few sharp barks. The sound
surprises you. You've never heard him bark before.

"What's the matter?" you ask, leaning down.
"Are you hungry already?"

To sit down on the rocks and feed Shadow, turn to page 61.

To investigate the area, turn to page 58.

You give the little pooch one last scratch on the head then shoo him off and go on your way. The dog follows you for another kilometre or so before finally disappearing over a jebel. For the next few kilometres, you find yourself scanning the horizon for a glimpse of him, but it's the last you see of him.

"Look at that," RJ says.

Ahead stands the biggest jebel yet. It's a rocky, craggy slope that would be a challenge even to a fresh runner. You and Mona both groan together. As you stand there looking up, another group passes you by.

"Should be the last one," calls out a man who introduces himself as Muhammad. He's a Moroccan native and knows the terrain. "You'll be in camp popping blisters in no time!"

With that, Muhammad's group starts up. You watch them ascend, carefully choosing their steps.

"Now or never," you say, leading the way.

At first, it's not as hard as it looks. But the slope grows steeper as you near the top. Suddenly, you hear RJ cry out. You whirl around to see him falling to the ground. He clutches his ankle, a grimace of pain on his face.

You and your sister rush to RJ's side.

"I think it's broken," Mona gasps.

The sun dips lower and lower. You're already close to the cut-off time. If RJ has a broken ankle, you'll have no chance of finishing the race.

"Go on ahead," Mona tells you. "I'll stay here with RJ."

To go on alone, turn to page 64.
To stay and help, turn to page 66.

RJ slides his rucksack off of his shoulders and gets ready to flop down onto one of the rocks. Shadow's barking grows louder as it grows more and more urgent.

"Hold on," you shout.

RJ freezes.

You approach the rocks carefully. A large crevice separates two of them. It's the exact spot where Shadow appears to be barking.

You kneel down for a closer look. You peer down into the crevice and then almost fall over backwards in your hurry to get away.

"Snake!" you shout. Everyone steps back as a long, pale figure darts out from the rock.

"That's a desert-horned viper," Mona gasps. "Its venom can be deadly."

The venomous desert-horned viper of
the Sahara is one tough customer.

The snake is poised to strike. You freeze in place, trying not to appear threatening to the snake. Unfortunately, Shadow does not. The little dog charges at the snake, barking at it fiercely.

It all happens in a flash. Shadow darting in at the snake. The viper striking. Shadow's pitiful whine as the snake slithers quickly across the desert sands.

Turn the page.

"Shadow!" you cry, rushing to his side.

The bite is on one of Shadow's front legs. He shakes and whimpers. RJ shouts for help.

You're in luck. A British TV crew covering the race isn't far away. They rush to you in their jeep, cameras rolling all the while.

"You've got to get him medical help right away," offers a reporter, who introduces herself as Susanna. "Come on, we'll take you."

"Wait," says RJ. "If you go, you'll be eliminated from the race!"

You look from your siblings to Shadow and back again. There's no time to debate.

To go with the TV crew, turn to page 68.
To finish the race, turn to page 71.

"What's got into that dog?" RJ asks as he pulls his canteen from his pack.

"I think maybe he's hungry," you answer. As you move towards the rocks, Shadow darts in front of you. You almost trip over him.

"Move, Shadow," you command, sitting down. But just as you do, a sharp, piercing pain shoots through your left leg.

You yelp in surprise as something long and brown shoots out from a crack in the rocks and slithers away. A snake!

"What was that?" you ask in a panic.

"I think it was a desert-horned viper," RJ says, his voice shaking. "Its venom can be deadly!"

Turn the page.

The desert-horned viper's venom can be fatal, and snakebite victims must seek medical attention.

Shadow keeps barking at the fleeing snake as you roll up your trouser leg. The skin shows twin punctures. It's red and swollen, and it stings like mad.

RJ strikes out for help. The last checkpoint was less than a kilometre away. You, Mona and Shadow wait together for a medical team to arrive. "Don't worry," Mona assures you. "They can treat this."

You're confident that you'll be okay. You'll be taken to a hospital and pulled from the race. You don't know what will happen to all the friends you've made. Mona says that she'll look after Shadow. "We'll find a way to get this little dog home with us," she promises. That does make you feel a little better. But it doesn't make up for one crushing fact: your adventure in the Sahara is over.

THE END

To follow another path, turn to page 11.
To learn more about the Marathon des Sables, turn to page 101.

You wish your siblings well and then strike out alone. Setting your own pace, you quickly scale the rest of the jebel. It's a downhill run to the finish line. The first thing you do is send for help. The medical team takes off. When RJ and Mona finally reach camp that night, your brother's ankle is in a boot. "We're going to take him by helicopter to a hospital," explains one of the nurses. "Your sister is going with him."

You stay back to finish the race. You spend the last three stages with Muhammad's group. They're good people and run at a comfortable pace for you. But you just can't enjoy yourself. Even as you finally cross the stage-six finish line, your thoughts turn to your brother.

You came to Morocco thinking that finishing the race was the only thing that mattered.

But as you watch the other racers celebrating, you feel no joy. And you realise that finishing the race wasn't really what you came for. You came to be with your siblings. As they've grown older, you've seen less and less of them. This may have been the last chance the three of you had to really have an adventure together.

THE END

To follow another path, turn to page 11.
To learn more about the Marathon des Sables, turn to page 101.

There's no way you're going to be running on ahead with RJ injured.

"We'll do this together," you say, slinging RJ's rucksack over your shoulder.

When you were 10, you fell on your bike and sprained your ankle. RJ carried you all the way home. There's no way you're leaving him here now.

You help RJ to his feet. He can't put any weight on his ankle, so you and Mona each support him on one side. He hops along, leaning on the two of you. It's only a kilometre to the finish line. But at this speed, it takes more than an hour. The three of you finish well past the cut-off time.

"I'm sorry," says a race official. "You didn't make it. This is the end of the race for you."

For a moment, you feel crushed. The three of you enter camp with you and Mona supporting RJ. As you make your way to the medical tent, your fellow racers all stand and applaud. It starts with a few claps. But as more and more racers see what's happening, it turns into a roar.

You didn't finish the Marathon des Sables. But with your siblings at your side, you feel like a winner today.

THE END

To follow another path, turn to page 11.
To learn more about the Marathon des Sables, turn to page 101.

Shadow has become your constant companion. He may have just saved your life. He needs help, and you're not going to leave his side. You agree to go with the TV crew, forfeiting your chance to complete the race.

The crew rushes ahead to the medical station at the end of the stage. The jeep rattles and rolls over the uneven terrain, kicking up clouds of dust.

Jeeps are a preferred method of transport in desert terrain.

Shadow is fading fast. He's silent now. He lies in your lap, trembling.

Once in camp, you waste no time. Within moments, two of the race's doctors are at work. By now, everyone at camp knows and loves Shadow – the race staff included. The TV cameras roll as the doctors frantically work on the little dog.

"I think he'll make it," says one of the doctors after several minutes. They've given him an antivenin to combat the venom. Shadow is sleeping peacefully, a bandage around the wound.

You stay there by his side until he wakes up, looks at you and gives you a weak lick across the hand. Over the next few hours, he grows stronger and stronger, until he's finally back up on his feet and eating again.

Turn the page.

While your siblings finish the race, you stay with Shadow, working to get permission to take him out of the country. There's no way you're leaving your friend behind.

Back home, part of you regrets not finishing the race. But you know it was well worth it. You went to finish one of the world's most extreme foot races. Instead, you came home with a new best friend. It's a good trade.

THE END

To follow another path, turn to page 11.
To learn more about the Marathon des Sables, turn to page 101.

"Take him," you tell Susanna. "Get him help. We'll see you, first thing, at the finish line for the stage."

You watch the jeep drive off, kicking up a trail of dust in its wake. And the three of you are off to finish the stage. You're distracted the entire way, though. All you can think about is Shadow. As you cross the stage's finish line, all you want to do is to check on your friend. But Shadow is nowhere to be found.

You spot Susanna and wave her down.

She rushes up to you. "Don't worry," she says. "Shadow will be okay. They treated him here, then sent him off to an animal shelter for care. I'm sure they'll find the little pooch a good home. I'll make sure of it."

Turn the page.

The desert can be a lonely place — even
for the furriest of four-legged friends.

Shadow remains in your thoughts as you
finish the race. The pain of your body dulls
when compared to how you feel about missing
your friend. After the race is over, Susanna and
the crew drive you to the animal shelter.

"I'm sorry," says one of the caretakers at the
shelter. "A family adopted that dog this morning.
Don't worry, he'll have a good home."

There's nothing more you can do. You're happy Shadow was adopted. But it breaks your heart that you never got to say goodbye. You've completed the Marathon des Sables. It's a wonderful feeling of accomplishment. Yet your enduring memory of your week in Morocco is the four-legged friend you left behind.

THE END

To follow another path, turn to page 11.
To learn more about the Marathon des Sables, turn to page 101.

CHAPTER 4

THE HOME STRETCH

Haley smiles as you trot over to join her and her father. You've always been a huge fan of an underdog story, and running with someone as courageous as Haley is a chance you can't pass up. Running with Haley will be a challenge. Your own race will be on the line if she's not up to it. But you believe in her, and you're willing to take that chance.

For the first four stages, you, Andrew and Haley constantly flirt with that cut-off time. During the race, they're serious runners – every kilometre is such a battle for Haley that there's not a lot of time for joking around.

Turn the page.

At camp, though, they're two of the most talkative and funny people you've ever met. In the brutal third leg, which takes you over mountain-covered terrain, you cross the finish line with less than 10 minutes to spare.

"Man, that was close," you say.

"We got lucky there," says Andrew.

Haley – the optimist of the group – flashes the two of you a smile. "Aw, stop it. We had 10 minutes to spare. Plenty of time."

The night before the fifth leg, you're in terrible pain. During the last stage, some sand got inside your socks and shoes. It rubbed against your skin, giving you a massive, oozing blister. But as you look over at Haley, you refuse to feel sorry for yourself.

Haley's feet are in even worse shape. Three of the toenails on her right foot have actually fallen off. You imagine that the pain must be excruciating, yet Haley never complains.

Stage five covers a wide and flat salt plain.

Desert landscapes include a vast variety of dunes and plains.

Turn the page.

The sun bakes the earth here. It's like running in an oven. As the three of you follow the tracks of the racers that came before you, your feet hurt more and more.

At one checkpoint, you find your socks spotted red with blood. A blister the size of a grape has grown on your big toe. It's oozing red-tinted fluid. Unfortunately you know what that means – you have an infection.

Everyone here is dealing with blisters and sore feet. Why should you be any different? You wrap your foot tight with athletic tape, slip your sock back on and painfully force your foot back inside your shoe.

You and Andrew take turns holding Haley's arm as you move, calling out any obstacles that appear in your way.

"Rock," you say, guiding her to the left. "A little dune coming up, now. Get ready for a climb."

You come into a series of low dunes. Despite the pain in your foot, you're feeling elated. You're getting so close now. You've watched some of your fellow racers charge down the dunes at top speed. It looks like fun, but you've never tried it.

To sprint down the dune, turn to page 98.
To continue on a slower pace, turn to page 80.

Now isn't the time to be careless. There's a long way to go and many kilometres to complete before it's time to play.

You fall into a rhythm ... step, step, step. It's almost hypnotic. Helping Haley is a good way to take your mind off your own challenges, even if Andrew does most of the work. As the day wears on, the sun grows hotter and hotter. All three of you are sweating heavily, and you notice that Andrew's face is very red.

You pass one checkpoint, then another. You're making progress, but a glance at your watch tells you that you're falling badly behind schedule. You need to pick up the pace if you're going to make it to the finish line before the cut off.

You're leading the way as the three of you climb a small jebel. You're stopped by a sudden shout from Haley. "Dad! DAD!"

You whirl around to see Andrew lying prone on the ground.

"What happened?" you cry as you hurry back.

Competitors in the Marathon des Sables encounter a wide variety of sand dunes.

Turn the page.

"I think he fainted," Haley replies, panic in her voice.

You grab your bottle and pour a bit of precious water on Andrew's face. He's burning up. His eyes flutter open and closed.

He mutters something that you can't really make out.

"I think it's heat stroke," you tell Haley. "We've got to try to keep him cool."

A large boulder rests just a metre away. Together, you help Andrew into what little shade it provides. Haley fans him with an extra shirt while you flag down a group not far behind. Within a few minutes, Andrew is conscious again, drinking water and looking more alert. But looking at him, you can tell he's not going anywhere soon.

The other group arrives and promises to send help. Another group passes you. "We'll send help," they promise. "There's a checkpoint less than two kilometres ahead."

Grimacing, Andrew looks at you. "Take Haley. Keep going. Please. Help will be along for me shortly."

"No way, Dad," Haley insists. "I'm not leaving you here alone."

"You don't have time," Andrew replies. "My race is over. But you two could still make it."

To continue on with Haley, turn to page 84.
To wait here until help arrives, turn to page 89.

Haley doesn't want to leave her dad behind, but the two of you finally convince her. "He came here for you," you remind her as the two of you say your goodbyes and continue along the track. "We can't let him down now."

The terrain of the Marathon des Sables is as sandy as it is challenging.

You have to give her credit. Haley is tough. She gets it, and once she commits to carrying on, she does it without regret. "We're going to have to move," she says. "I know we're cutting it close."

That's exactly what you do. You pick up your pace, crossing another oven-hot salt flat, scaling several dunes and ticking off one checkpoint after the next. You finally hobble across the finish line, side by side, with only minutes to spare. Andrew is already at camp, getting treatment for heat stroke. He'll be fine, but his race is over.

One stage remains. After a day of rest, you'll be on your way to the greatest accomplishment of your life. But the first thing you need to do is have your feet examined. The queue for medical care wraps around the medical tent. Everyone is suffering. You wait for more than an hour until it's your turn.

Turn the page.

You know that the doctors have seen just about every kind of foot injury they can see, but the young woman inspecting your foot still winces at the sight of your big, bulging blister.

"It's infected," she explains. "I'll give you some antibiotics and painkillers. But you should really stop and think about whether you want to go on. Another day out there could make this much worse. If that infection were to get into the bone, you could be risking the loss of your foot."

That's not the news you want to hear. Part of you is ready to give up. You've managed to survive five-sixths of the race already. Is it really that important to complete just one more stage? Is it worth risking an infection that could affect your long-term health?

To continue the race, turn to page 87.
To call it a day and protect your health, turn to page 91.

Dawn before the final stage stirs up some intense feelings.

You watch the sun rise over the eastern horizon, knowing that it will be your final day. The last stage is the shortest of the race. On paper, it looks like the easiest.

For the first few kilometres, you and Haley manage to keep a modest pace. She could go faster, but your feet are in such pain that all you can do is hobble along.

It's just after the first checkpoint when things start to go downhill for you. The pain in your foot seems to grow with each step. It feels like something worse than just a blister. You worry that the infection may have spread deeper. If it gets to the bone, you could have serious trouble.

Turn the page.

A fellow racer sees your struggle. She approaches you and introduces herself. "I'm Sandra," she says, digging into her pack. She pulls out a sturdy, collapsible walking stick. "You look like you could use this."

It's a walking stick, but you know that if you use it, it will be as a crutch. The image of you crossing the finish line while leaning on a crutch is not what you had in mind.

To take the stick, turn to page 93.

To try to finish without the help, turn to page 95.

"I don't care about our time at the moment," you tell Andrew, flopping down next to him.

You would have thought that getting off your feet would feel good. But stopping here allows you to focus on the pain. You can't imagine how Andrew must be hurting.

It's close to an hour before a medic arrives.

She confirms your fears. "You're suffering from heat stroke," she tells Andrew. "Even now, you're body is struggling to maintain its temperature. We have to evacuate you and get you treatment."

"I'm coming with you, Dad," Haley says. She turns to you. "I'm so sorry," she says, choking back tears. "You should go now. Maybe you can still make it in time."

Turn the page.

There's nothing left for you to do here.

You give your new friends hugs, wish them luck and then start off into the desert on your own. It's a long, excruciating day. You push yourself as hard as you can, but you know it's hopeless.

Mona and RJ are there to greet you at the finish line. Of course, it's far too late – you cross well past the cut-off time. Your race has come to an end.

THE END

To follow another path, turn to page 11.
To learn more about the Marathon des Sables, turn to page 101.

Enough is enough, you decide. You came out here to conquer the desert, and you feel like you've done that already. What's the point of endangering your health just to say you finished?

"I think it's time to bow out," you tell the woman. She gives you a long look and then nods. She seems sad to hear it but agrees that it's the most sensible decision.

Participants in the Marathon des Sables occasionally stop to rest and take in the magnificent beauty of the Sahara.

Turn the page.

Haley breaks down in tears when you tell her the news. You realise that your decision hasn't just affected you. With you and Andrew both out of the race, Haley won't be getting her chance to finish either.

Mona wraps you up in a hug when you tell her. RJ tries to talk you into changing your mind. He seems disgusted that you'd give up after all this. But your mind is made up. You've had enough of the Marathon des Sables. And finishing five-sixths of the race is almost as good as finishing the whole thing.

Isn't it?

THE END

To follow another path, turn to page 11.
To learn more about the Marathon des Sables, turn to page 101.

You've just spent a week racing across the desert. Haley has been at your side every step of the way, and she's done it all without the ability to see. What difference does it make if you use a crutch as long as you make it?

You accept the walking stick from Sandra with thanks. It takes a bit to get the hang of using it, all while helping Haley. But soon, you've got it down.

Step by painful step, the two of you make your way over the desert sands.

Turn the page.

The aid of a walking stick can be a big advantage in rough desert terrain.

At first, other racers pass you by, wishing you luck. Soon, nobody is left to pass you. You and Haley are dead last among the remaining racers.

"It doesn't matter where we finish," Haley reminds you. "All that matters is that we finish."

Hour after hour passes. For everyone else, the race is long over. But many of the racers stay behind. They erupt in cheers as you rise above the final dune and limp across the finish line. Among them are many of the friends you've made along the way – Andrew, Gunther, Zelig, and of course, your brother and sister. The grin on Haley's face makes it all worthwhile.

"We did it," she cries as she hugs you. You can hardly believe it yourself.

THE END

To follow another path, turn to page 11.
To learn more about the Marathon des Sables, turn to page 101.

You're almost there. Just a bit more than twelve kilometres to go. You've come this far, and you're not going to rely on a crutch now. "No thanks," you say. "I'll be all right."

Sandra shrugs and charges ahead. You and Haley plod along. You keep waiting for the pain to fade as it has during other stages. But it just gets worse and worse.

You come to the race's final checkpoint, the last of the racers to pass through.

The young doctor you saw last night is waiting there. "We heard you might be in some trouble," she says.

"I'm fine," you insist. But even as you speak the words, a wave of dizziness sweeps over you. Your knees buckle and you collapse to the ground in an exhausted heap.

Turn the page.

The doctor and the rest of the medical team are there straight away. Everything is garbled and confusing. Your mind just isn't working right. You pick out bits and pieces of what they're saying… very low blood pressure … extreme dehydration … aggressive infection … call for air evacuation.

For extreme cases of injury or illness, runners may be evacuated by helicopter at the Marathon des Sables.

None of it makes sense to you. Even as they load you onto a helicopter for a medical evacuation, you don't really realise that you're no longer fighting to finish the race. Now, you're fighting for your life. You can only hope this fight ends with a better result.

THE END

To follow another path, turn to page 11.
To learn more about the Marathon des Sables, turn to page 101.

"What the heck," you mutter to yourself. You're out here, and you may never be back. Right now, all you want to do is charge down a sand dune.

You start to sprint. It's exciting. The desert breeze rushes past your face. Sand kicks up behind your feet as you go faster and faster. You raise your arms and let out a loud woo hoo!

Runners must use extreme caution at all times when crossing large sand dunes.

Then it all goes wrong. You're going fast – too fast. Suddenly, your feet can't keep up with your body. You tumble headfirst into the sand, throwing your arms out to try to catch yourself. You hear a SNAP as you hit the ground. You cry out in pain as you skip and bounce your way down the rest of the dune, crashing at the bottom with a thump.

Your left arm hangs limp at your side. You can't even lift it. Andrew and Haley arrive as quickly as they can to help you. You manage to stand and hobble to the next checkpoint. But your arm is fractured. Your race is over. And you know that as long as you live, you'll never sprint down another sand dune.

THE END

To follow another path, turn to page 11.
To learn more about the Marathon des Sables, turn to page 101.

CHAPTER 5

THE MARATHON OF THE SANDS

The Marathon des Sables is one of the most difficult and extreme athletic competitions in the world. This six-day, 251-kilometre (156-mile) "ultra marathon" stacks about six full marathons into seven days (six legs with one day of rest). And it takes place on one of the world's harshest landscapes – Morocco's Sahara Desert.

The event's origins trace back to 1984. That was when French concert promoter Patrick Bauer packed his things and headed out, on foot and alone, into the Sahara. Bauer spent 12 days crossing the desert. The experience moved him to bring the experience to others.

And so Bauer set up the first Marathon des Sables in 1986. The event attracted 186 adventurous competitors. French racers won both the men's and women's divisions. Michel Galliez and Christiane Plumere became the first Marathon des Sables champions.

Over the decades, Bauer saw his race grow and grow. The race has become a truly international affair. France dominated the competition early on. The nation's runners swept the event in each of the first six runnings. Mohamed Bensalah of Morocco broke that streak in 1992. Since then, locals have taken over, especially in the men's division. The most successful racer in history is Morocco's Lahcen Ahansal. He has won the event 10 times. His brother Mohamad Ahansal has added three more titles to the family name.

Today, more than a thousand people flock to Morocco to compete annually. Most train for many months to prepare for the race. They pack their supplies carefully, knowing that they have to carry everything they might need.

Climbing, as well as running or walking, is an important skill to possess for Marathon des Sables competitors.

And they spend thousands upon thousands of pounds in gear, travel expenses and the race's entry fee. Yet despite the investments of time, energy and money, few of those who run the race are there with the goal of winning. Rather, for most, it's about personal challenge and overcoming incredible odds. Just finishing at all is the biggest goal.

The Sahara gives the race its character. It is a harsh, unforgiving land, filled with beauty and danger – from the sight of rocky jebels rising above the desert sands to the constant threats of dehydration, heat stroke and encounters with deadly desert creatures such as snakes and scorpions.

Racers and organizers are careful to leave the desert as they find it. They leave nothing behind but tracks. Racers receive time penalties for leaving behind even the tiniest bit of litter It's all a part of the race's culture to preserve the unique environment that makes the race the one-of-a-kind spectacle that it is.

DANGERS of the DESERT

Extreme heat

Extreme heat is a weather event that kills thousands of people each year. It is especially dangerous in the desert climate of the Sahara. Dehydration and heat stroke are dangers to avoid. Dehydration occurs when the amount of water exiting the body is greater than the amount going in. Symptoms of heat stroke are confusion, agitation, disorientation, lack of sweating and in extreme cases, coma.

Sandstorms

Sandstorms whip up heaps of sand and dust that can rise to be over 300 metres (10,000 feet) tall. Their wind speeds can range from 40–60 kilometres (25–100 miles) per hour. Dust from the Sahara Desert has been known to blow over the oceans to Europe and other parts of the world.

Venomous snakes

The two most dangerous snakes in the Sahara Desert are the horned-desert viper and the saw-scaled viper. They often bury themselves in sand to keep cool but can also be found in burrows during the winter months.

Other dangerous animals

The deathstalker scorpion can be nearly 10 centimetres (4 inches) in length. It has dangerous venom with large amounts of poison. Jackals and hyenas also roam the Sahara.

GLOSSARY

antibiotic   drug that kills bacteria

barren   producing little or no vegetation

canteen   small, durable water bottle

dehydration   condition in which the body doesn't have enough water to carry out its basic functions

delusion   mistaken or misleading belief

dune   ridge of sand piled up by the wind

embassy   official residence or offices of an ambassador to another nation

evacuate   leave a dangerous place to go somewhere safer

excruciating   causing great mental or physical pain

fracture   break or crack in something, such as a bone

heat stroke   condition caused by overheating, in which the body loses its ability to regulate its own temperature. Heat stroke causes fever and loss of consciousness, and can lead to death.

hobble   walk with difficulty

horizon   line where the sky and the Earth or sea seem to meet

hypnotic   tending to cause a sleep-like state

jebel   Middle-Eastern term for a hill or mountain

marathon   long-distance race that takes place over 42.2 kilometres (26 miles, 385 yards)

optimistic   expecting everything to come out all right

ration   set amount of something allotted to a person each day

sibling   brother or sister

terrain   surface of the land

OTHER PATHS TO EXPLORE

❖ One of the characters you encountered in your
  Marathon des Sables journey was Haley, who
  is blind. How different might the experience be
  for someone with a disability such as blindness
  or deafness? What additional challenges would
  a person face with such a disability, and how
  might one overcome them?

❖ The Marathon des Sables takes runners
  through many parts of the Sahara, including
  areas where people live. What would it be like
  to watch the race as a Moroccan child? Would
  it make you want to run it yourself one day? Or
  would you think that even trying such a feat is
  mad? How would you feel about the runners
  coming to your home country to race?

❖ The Sahara is one of the world's most extreme
  environments. What other challenging settings
  might make for an interesting endurance
  race? Are there places in the world where the
  conditions would be just too harsh for such an
  event to ever take place?

FIND OUT MORE

BOOKS

Morocco (Cultures of the World), Pat Seward
(Cavendish Square Publishing, 2016)

Trekking the Sahara Desert (Travelling Wild), Sonya
Newland (Wayland, 2016)

You Choose: Surviving Mount Everest (You Choose:
Surviving Extreme Sports), Blake Hoena
(Raintree, 2017)

WEBSITES

www.dkfindout.com/uk/earth/deserts
Find out all about deserts on this website.

www.marathondessables.com/en/marathon-des-sables-maroc/history
This web page tells the history of the Marathon des
Sables and lists all the previous winners.

INDEX